PAINKILLERS: ADVENTURES IN DYSTOPIA

POEMS

JABEZ VAN CLEEF

PAINKILLERS

Painting on cover by Jane H. Van Cleef.

Books by Jabez L. Van Cleef

Secular Poetry and Fiction

Painkillers
Heaven On Earth
It Rhymes With Breath:
Five Stories of Death
Trust Me On This One:
Three Stories of Betrayal
Children of Wrath
Left Eye/Right Eye & Into My Belly
Real Corkers: Stories for Children

PAINKILLERS

Other Books by Jabez L. Van Cleef

On Mysticism
in the Anglican Tradition

The Song of the Cloud of Unknowing
The Song of the Showing of Love
The Song of the Fire of Love

On Human Rights
and Civil Disobedience

The Palimpsest of Human Rights
The Song of the Captives
All One Family Sing &
The Birth of Propaganda

Verse Adaptations
of Judeo-Christian Texts

Gospels in Verse
The Saxon Gospel
Strength In Trembling
Four Liturgical Plays

On World Religions
and Indigenous Cultures

All Is Beautiful:The Navajo Creation Story
God Wears Many Skins
He Kumulipo
The Tawasin of Mansur al-Hallaj
The Alchemy of Happiness
The Unstruck Drum of Eternity:
Poetry of Kabir
The Song of Confucius
Igbo Singing, & Three Igbo Stories
Nanai & The Quest for the Fire Bird

PAINKILLERS

PAINKILLERS

A SPIRITUAL
RESOURCE FOR
SUSTAINABLE LIVING
POETRY BY
JABEZ L. VAN CLEEF

Copyright © 2008
Jabez L. Van Cleef

Published by
Spirit Song Text Publications
20 Pine Avenue
Madison, New Jersey 07940
www.sustainyourspirit.com

Library of Congress
Cataloging-in-Publication Data
Painkillers: Adventures In Dystopia
Poems by Jabez L. Van Cleef
ISBN   1438229747   (paper).
EAN-13   9781438229744
I. Van Cleef, Jabez L. 1948-   . II. Title
2 4 6 8 9 7 5 3
Printed in the United States of America

PAINKILLERS

PAINKILLERS: ADVENTURES IN DYSTOPIA

PAINKILLERS

For Dan Karger.

PAINKILLERS

Introductory Note

The theory behind writing these poems is that if you are feeling miserable, and you write about how you are feeling, with as much precision and thoroughness as you can muster, you will induce in yourself a kind of satisfaction that you are able to make something worthwhile emerge from the misery.

The theory behind publishing these poems is that if someone else with similar feelings to your own comes along and reads about these painful states of mind, that person may also come to feel a little better, either from understanding or a general sense of companionship.

PAINKILLERS

1. **It Could Be Worse**

It could be worse

It is worse
right now
for somebody, somewhere

The one in the chair
isn't there
by choice

The one
with the drill isn't
charging
a
fee

Someone in a uniform
writes
a check

You don't have to tell us
which one
of your
fami-
ly

Is plot-
ting to
over-
throw the re-

gime, all

You
have to do is

Sit still

And ac-
cept the treatment you
asked for

Afterward you will feel better

In a few
days you will for-
get what
it felt like al-

together

2. Management Of The Pain

You can make op-
timum use of the pain
you are in by imag-
ining that each wave
is bright redyellow
bluegreen sand pouring a
painting up inside a
clear plastic squeeze-
toy making overlapping
stripes along the side until when it's full you can
screw on the head and
grab the body as hard as you
can
with both hands at once
and squeeeeeeeeze it, I said
really squeeeeeeeeeeze it, and
squeezitandsqueezitandsqueez
it
about a hundred times
until all the tiny little
grains of different colored
sand are mixed up together.

PAINKILLERS

3.   **What It Is**

Pain is
what we call
our body's way of
bringing
its own conscious-
ness
of itself into
the most immediate
possible
in-
stant of
the present.

The sud-
den sharp
intake
of the breath
tells the
deeper ear behind
the sound to
listen.

If, in
fact the
heart
still beats
it will noti-
fy the proper
authorities. And

Through channels
word comes that
other
senses may be called in
to assess what is
meant by this
now.

4.   **A Major Obstacle**

In dealing
with
my pain
as with many other things
I find
the thing that
most often gets
in
my way
is me.

PAINKILLERS

5.   **Separated At Birth**

I have questions
about
what people call pain
and the same (or
other) people
call pleasure.

Is it a matter of
degree, more
neurons firing
or something?

Are there different nerve
cells at work sens-
ing or
a different network
of strands con-
veying the electro-
chemical impulses?

Is it pro-
cessed in a different
part
of the brain?

Is there any
agreement
about which
is which among
different people?

If we are taught
to differ-
entiate pain
from
pleasure as we grow,
does that mean
we dis-
tinguish pain
from an over-
all sensation of pleasure
or vice-
versa?

6.   **Doctors & Dentists**

Doctors & Dentists
are
trained
to see our pain
from above
and treat it
(and us)
objectively.

That means they
make believe we are
inanimate objects or
sources of data inas-
much as they need to
diagnose
the cause of the
pain.

They would agree that
pain is needed for our
survival,
that it is
not normal
to be without pain,

As important in its way
as the spine or the
tooth.

PAINKILLERS

7.   **Many Are The Alcoholics**

Many are the alcoholics
who say
they finally stopped
when the pain
of continuing
proved to be greater
than the pain
of stopping.

It reminds me
of what Einstein said
after Hiro-
shima:

"The bomb
has changed everything
except
our way of thinking."

PAINKILLERS

8.   **The Western Model**

The western model
of medical practice
sees
the disease as
a target, the
profession
as a gun
and the
treatment
as a
bullet.

The practitioner
pulls
the trigger.

With some
kinds of pain
the moment
the pathologic
agent or
symptom is
aligned with the
crosshairs, it
dis-
appears.

There ought to be
another
treatment model, or
for that matter,
many.

9.   Investment

I don't think you can
understand dental pain
unless you first under-
stand
why children don't like
to brush their teeth.

Years of nagging,
and the suspicion that maybe
they were right
all the time,
contribute to my otherwise
adult
approach to personal care.

Consider also that a tooth
does not heal, and
it belongs to the same family
as my skeletal remains,
and you can understand
something about
my reluctance to schedule
dental appoint-
ments
when I should.

Each tooth
I have lost is a
small brick
in the wall of my mortality.

PAINKILLERS

9.   A Logical Question

If
you
have
left
behind
your
fear
of
dying
can
your
fear
of
pain
survive?

PAINKILLERS

10.   **A Hole In The Ground**

Lucy gets into my lap
at the Friendly's after the
hamburger
but before the mint
chocolate chip.

Is she curling up for a nap
or what?

She was the one who slept
all the way through
 every night
but in the afternoon,
forget it.
That's ancient history now
she's seven
or is it?
I think as her head bores
into my chest,
about her elbows
and how sharp they are.

Daddy, she says into the cloth,
I don't want you to die. Why
do I hear such a good humor
lurking in her muffled voice?

I wasn't thinking about it,
I told her,

PAINKILLERS

I don't want you to die either,
not today at least.

Later we went for a walk
in the Great Swamp
Wildlife Refuge.
We saw two smallish bunnies
waddling off the path
and into their
hole in the ground.
You know Lucy, I said
not thinking about what she
had said before
but just making talk,
There's really no reason
to be afraid of the dark.
Look at those bunnies.
When they're home
it's dark all the time.

11. **Living In The Pain**

This is what I want.

I want my eyes to be so sharp
and open and alert
they trace the edge of
each leaf in
the maple I walk by
at daybreak.

I want my ears to hear
each stroke of a bird's wing
even a hummingbird's wing,
even a mosquito,
and even so
at the same time follow
the sluggish progress of
blood in my
intestines.

Can you imagine
this hand of mine
covered front and back with
cats' whiskers?
They arch out every
whichway, quivering as if each
sensitive tendril knows that it
will be the next one to flick.

That's how ready I want my
sense of touch to be,

even when I am sleeping.

And hey, there are smells I
remember from before I
remember anything
that I still
haven't thought of a name for.

When I go to sleep at night, I
lie in bed and wish that my
tongue and the inside of me
knew what I really taste like
instead of what I think I taste
like.

Whatever combination of these
my senses,
these ways of knowing,
these me's,
it takes
to feel my pain,
I hope they're still working,
then

Because if I'm getting ready
to die,
I want to know what's
happening.

12.   Adam Named The Animals

During the still unknown
period when God had made Adam but
not yet Eve,
Adam named the animals. It is
the first deed of someone besides
God in the story
of creation.

We have the gift of artifice and
simulation.

Sometimes I think that human history
is nothing more than
the a continuous collective effort to
create better duplicates of our own
conscious experience,

Which some would say is only
a poor imitation of God's conscious
experience.

The God of the Hebrews bears the
name of a total present and fulfilled
consciousness:

I AM THAT I AM.

Human beings have brought this idea
down to earth in many ways.

When we ask, Are you who you say
you are? or, if the question is really
important, Are you who you are? the
question is about authenticity.
When we ask, Do you really mean
that? the question is about sincerity.

These are not just words.

People spend more money on things
because they believe them to have
more of the What-ness called Qual-
ity.

We are seeking something. We are
seeking a thing that is exactly what it is
and not something else.

(You shall have no other gods besides me.)

It is not both here and also there.

(Lucy said to me,
Daddy, when I look at the wheel turning
on a car going by, it goes faster the closer
you get to the edge of the wheel.
True, I said.
It goes slower as you look at it towards the
center of the wheel.
True, I said.
So, in the very very center of the wheel,
there must be a teeny little spot where the
wheel isn't moving at all, right?

I don't know, I said.)

It is not both now and also then.

(John 8.58 Before Abraham was, I am.)

So what is it? The best all those books
can tell us is that we don't have the
capacity to understand what it is but
we have to keep trying.

I remember talking to my friend Bob
about suicide.

Bob, I close my eyes and I see the
whole world slowly spinning around a
huge vortex, an endless deep pit, and
inside it there is an enormous gaping
mouth opening and closing and I
slowly begin to understand that this
mouth is screaming out all the pain of
the universe, screaming and screaming
the pain, but it has no voice, it has no
way to release itself, it just opens and
no voice comes out..

And Bob says,

You have to love that place in yourself.
Spend some more time there.
You know what I mean?

PAINKILLERS

13.   **Many Different Ways**

escaping the pain
employing the pain

1) part-time
2) as an hourly employee
3) as a salaried employee
4) as a consultant on retainer

subduing the pain
delaying the pain

(only until you get home)

devouring the pain
cheering for the pain
eating the pain
sipping the pain
probing at the pain with the tip
of the
                    tongue

obeying the pain
embracing the pain
defying the pain
spreading dried hot peppers
on the pain like a slice of pizza

PAINKILLERS

14.   **Three Cheers For The Pain**

WHAT ARE WE GONNA
DO WITH IT
WHAT ARE WE GONNA
DO WITH IT
WHAT ARE WE GONNA
DO WITH IT

booma laka booma laka
siss boom bah

I've got something stuck in my
eye

I've got a pain
where the sun don't shine,
Don't tell me yours is
bigger than mine

rah rah ree
kick him in the knee
rah rah rass
kick him in the other knee

gimme a P,
gimme an A,
gimme an I,
gimme an N,

Whaddaya got?

LOUDER
LOUDER

(repeat from the beginning)

15. Sometimes You Can't See It If It's Right In Front Of You

I was thinking about this time I was
working in New York and one day
somebody came and told me to go see
the boss in his office and I though
O NO what is it this time what did I do
what is he going to do fire me and so I
slunk down the hall and went in to see
the boss it was about ten thirty in the
morning and he asked me to sit down
and he told me that he was really
pleased with the job I was doing and
the clients were really happy with my
work and he really didn't want me to
think that I wasn't appreciated and just
to show his appreciation what he was
going to do was give me a raise
effective with the next pay period and
it would be six, it would be six
thousand dollars but also since we
were approaching the end of the year
and he knew that my work had made
an important contribution to the great
year we had been having he was also
going to make sure that I got a good
christmas bonus so he was going to
also give me a bonus of another six, six
thousand dollars effective with the pay
period just before christmas so how
did I like it? I said I liked it fine, I

really did and I was glad to be working
in a place where they appreciated the
hard work that people did and in the
back of my mind I was wondering if
somebody had told him I was looking
for a job and he was trying to hold onto
me and wondering how that could be
because I wasn't looking for a job just
then I mean I had been about eight
months before but I had stopped and I
wondered if somebody did tell him
who it could have been as I walked out
the door of his office. But then I could
not wait to get my coat on and get
outside. I practically broke the down
button in the elevator I was in such a
hurry to get downstairs and into the
street. I was driven. I was bumping
into people in the street. There was
this ferocious deep unrest in the
middle of my chest until I could get
down there and into this bar on eighth
avenue I used to go to there, it was an
incredibly sleazy blarneystone with all
these old guys lined up along the bar
and stalagmites growing up out of the
bottom of the urinal that still worked,
and I really could not wait to get in
there and start putting a shot a beer a
shot a beer a shot a beer a shot a beer
like that inside of myself while I just
flicked the ashes off my cigarette and
wait for the big ball of buzz to radiate

out around me from my head which took a total of about two hours. Then I went back to work and found out we had a client visiting us that afternoon and the conference room was unbelievably hot I was sitting right by the radiator and the next thing you know I fell asleep right in the meeting and they couldn't even wake me up so they just left me sitting there and I came to at about 7:30 that evening and went home, and the next morning the boss told me I could keep the raise but he was damned if he was giving me a bonus after that performance.

PAINKILLERS

16.   Twenty Below

Beyond Bilwaggy Bay,
where Champlain lay
like a corridor between the mountains
rather solid than high,
and at midday
the mist rose thick
from the cold tin water,
and above the sheer twisting strength
of the juniper roots in the rusty rocks,
above the scarred ankles
of the ashes in the scree,
behind the whitestalked
redtipped thrill
of the birches
and the sumac's rose offertory,
the furzy billows of the foothills
and the hemlock's black feathers,
over gullies littered with twisted
trunks, broken elms,
and the nest of the tent caterpillar,
the sky blazed blue
like an alcohol flame
exploding each instant
without stopping
under the lens of the sun,
sheet upon sheet of white
and blue and white;
and there in a forest
flooded with ice
that had thrust the trees up

out of the ground,
by a brown cowtrod swamp
and patches
of sharp yellow grass,
under the sere leaves
of an oak
cracked and fluttering with frost,
stood an apple,
split midtrunk and screeching
noiselessly
under the burning sky
with the fingers of its branches
in the soil;
and majesty of majesties,
a house with a cupola
sat abandoned and windowless
in sight of the mountains
more solid than high,
revealing beneath a peeling of paint
and behind each shut shutter,
the secret
of the mysterious tenacity
of the apple.

17. You Name It

(Oh come on.

You can't mean to tell me
You never felt a thing
Painful enough
To have a need to write it down
So you could look at it later
And remember
Why it hurt, that it hurt,
And that it wasn't hurting so much
Any more.)

PAINKILLERS

18.   Has He Matured?

Has he matured? Is what
he does suitable
for society now
that he is married with
a child already and
responsibilities?
Will the baby, the
first one, understand if
these things intrude in
that way they have of intruding
when some more years go by and
the past refuses in its way to be
discarded?
Who could resist these
assertions that emerge encased in
their own energy
from that peculiar time in the
morning when he faces
himself in the mirror and
applies the razor to his cheek?
Even if he knows that in five
minutes he will be kissing
the baby's cheek, is
that enough to obliterate
the malingering of these memories?
Why, precisely, then, does
that image of his solitude, that
bundled lassitude and urgency of
his desperate, solitary being, come
to suggest itself as an ultimate

choice?

19.   Sheep Singing

Today
the clouds float in their field of
endless blue,
big clouds,
showing gray patches
along their underbellies,
shreds tearing off,
lingering on the tufts
of upwardly impinging air,
clouds that creep, as if
they had a guilty conscience
about throwing down all that water
on us yesterday,
as if they wanted to go hide
somewhere
but there is such a crowd of them,
jostling into the trough
of the horizon,
without even the outlet of a bleat;
they think they have no place to go.

O sheepish clouds,
go ye in your herds
to all your foolish places.
Find your voice and
sing your song to me:
voices meek,
trying both to speak
and to restrain the speaking,
to lift the line of song

and yet to chop
the words, like bits of burr or thistle.
Your hot brains, trapped
in narrow skulls,
what can they be thinking,
to launch
these tight little,
high little oboe sounds
with glottal stops between?

Begin, with your voiced labials,
yet begin
with certain restraint
holding back that voice;
not pushing, propelling,
but held back, becoming
for both sheep and humankind,
creeping in herds
toward that certain horizon,
an unfinished assertion of innocence
for the purging of the flood,
the surging of the blood.

20.   Jug Rap

When I was a little boy
Stung by a bee
Or when my older brother
Got ahold of me
I could feel my pain
I could feel my hurt
And out from my eyes
The tears would start to squirt
They would run so hot
They would stream so long
I couldn't say a word
I couldn't sing a song
So I opened my eyes
And I looked all around
To see what I could see
While the tears ran down
And lo and behold
Everything looked blurry
The people were blobs
The trees were all furry
But the best thing was
About looking through tears
It made the world look good
It took away my fears
It made me feel strong
Like I could deal with it
Showed me something down inside
Taught me how to feel with it.

But then one day my brothers

PAINKILLERS

Were drinkin down some booze
Said Come on little brother
Nothin here to lose
The stuff inside this bottle
Make you feel real good
Make you the star
Of the whole neighborhood
I always tried to do
What my brothers did too
And especially so
When they would tell me no
I could tell they liked it
The stuff inside the jug
So I took it from their hand
And stuck it in my mug
And it tasted real bad
But I drank it anyway
In about an hour
There was all hell to pay
Then my ears were buzzin
Then my eyes were crossed
Saw two of everything
As I turned and I tossed
Then my older brothers
They started to worry
Better get him sobered up
In a big hurry
Snuck into the house
With a great big thermos
Brought me some coffee
To stick inside my dermis
I drank it all down
Though I hated the taste

And it kept me awake
To experience the waste
Tasted so bad
I puked in the gutter
Talked with a honk
And a yelp and a stutter
The thing I meant to say
Was the very next morning
It came into my head
Without any warning
That any time I needed
To blur reality
I could find some beer or wine
To get inside of me.

When I had these feelings
I didn't want to feel
I would find a way
I would beg borrow steal
I would get a bottle
A bottle just for me
Or I would steal a nip
From the little pantry
There was always plenty
With the Old Man around
I got what I needed
My feelings I would drown.

As the years go by
You don't even see
That drinkin all the time
Is your everyday reality
That everything you do

Is aiming at the hour
When you can kick back
And feel the liquor power
You choose all your friends
To help you drink in peace
You make all your plans
You twist realities
The next thing you know
You've busted your bubble
No matter how far you go
You're bound to find some trouble
Trouble with the law
Trouble with money
Trouble with yourself
That's the kind that's not funny
You wake up some night
Some morning, two thirty
Can't get to sleep
Your brain's feelin dirty
Can't talk to anyone
Can't think what to say
Can't go anywhere
Got no games to play
So sorry this is happening
Hope you have a nice day
Then you start to wonder
Look inside the mirror
How you gonna deal
With this new world of terror
What you gonna do
When you feel the shaky hand
Where is the way
What's the lay of the land?

PAINKILLERS

Then you realize
That with all of these fears
Since you let the tears come
It's been twenty years
Your tears wash away
The feeling of dirt
Your tears can help you understand
Why you're feeling hurt
If you don't cry some tears
The feeling builds up
And you will find a time and place
To make a big PICK-UP
So you may try to stop
And you may try to quit
But all of your will power
Ain't worth a s---
Unless you can find a way
A way to admit
That when it comes to booze
Every day, every hour
You're only gonna lose
You ain't got the power
The booze is your master
You haven't got a clue
Your life is a mess
So what you gonna do
Gonna STOP every day
Sniff a little flower
Get down on your knees
And find your higher power
Don't take a drink
One day at a time

PAINKILLERS

Is the easiest way
To make your life rhyme.

21.   As It Should Be

The cut leaf maple
in the front
held its leaves
for the longest time
but last night
that hard frost
made all the grass
white
and now
as the bright sun
comes on strong
it melts the frost
on the higher leaves
and the weight of the water
breaks them loose
so they fall
one by one
and cover
the frozen grass
with red.

PAINKILLERS

22. Nautilus

From the place where my ear rests
in the pillow, and my other ear hears
steps outside the door, stepping
up and down, back and forth,
fugitive reports of life's pressure
against the incurious inanimate wood
and stone;

from that place, where I can only hear,
and today haven't mustered courage to
answer with either words or motions,
these importunities;

I find myself, catch myself, surveying
an inward vista, a spiral place,
heading down and in, and thanking
heaven I didn't break the spell of it
by opening my eyes.

Instead, as I held this inner place
firm before my attention, another part
of my thought,

another voice, was making plans for
me to secure a protected time and
sanction, somewhere in the
future of my day, perhaps the
following day,

when I would come back into this bed,

cover myself completely and banish
the light,
banish it all down to black,

and push the point of my awareness
down and in,

and where that spiral vessel would
hold me safe

against the particulate falling,

drifting

words.

23.   **In Your Eye**

You think you know
what's going to happen.
You don't know shit.
You know what I can do to you?
I can take these kids, and keep them.
I can take them and make sure you
never see them.

I can do whatever I want with them, I
can move to California.

You probably think I'm going to hit
you now.

I can see you getting ready to flinch.

I'm not getting ready to hit you.

I don't want to hit you.

I'll tell you what I want.

I want to kill you, that's what I want.
I want to make your shitty little face
disappear under the dirt.

You cringe, you go hide. You run
away now, big boy.

You get away from me.

PAINKILLERS

I'll stay here. I'll keep this house.
You'll pay for this.
You can go fuck yourself.
You can't look me in the eye, can you?

I know why.
You have a guilty conscience.

You're sorry for all those terrible things
you did, boo hoo hoo.

I'm not sorry. I'm glad.
I can't wait to get you out of my sight
and out of my life.

You listen good, this is your last
chance, don't ask me any more.
You're so fucking clueless, this is it,
you jerk.

I'm doing you a big favor, my precious
little jerkoff.
I'm not going discuss it any more.

You're history.

23.   Opening The Eyes

Somebody must have studied this:
I read somewhere
Where people who commit sui8cide,
Their children
Are supposed to be
so much more likely
To commit sui8cide,
Some particular amount,
some average
Percentage or
something.

I read this somewhere.
But what I want to know
Is if you look at the real lives
of the people
What happens?

I mean, I have to live with my father
's memory, of how
He used to just sit there
and drink all day

Manhattans
Whiskey and ginger ale
Fleischmann's on the rocks

(my Mother told me the same company
made the
little packages of yeast)

And after many years of doing that
and
Smoking a couple of packs of Camels
or Chesterfields
And some crossword puzzles
Black and white television
Candling eggs
Bawling us out
for being pigs and slobs,
He had to go in for an operation
Aneurysm in the aorta
Which they fixed

But they told my Mother
he really only could hope for
five more years
at the most

And even though he didn't know that
(did he know that?)
Maybe he did
But I don't think it matters
Because he didn't quit

He hid the bottles and the cigarettes
out in the garage
Or elsewhere,

He would get into a fight with her
And storm out the back, saying
This is it, I might as well end it all

PAINKILLERS

Once and for all

And she would wait for him
to come back

Sometimes he didn't come back
She went looking for him

She found him in the garage
Passed out on the floor with the
empty bottle next to him
And some burnt out butts

Asleep

And she couldn't wake him up
Or carry him in
So she went and found a blanket

Covered him

And left him on the concrete.

I didn't see that part
But I saw plenty.

And then when I grew up
I had the chance

(I made the chance myself,
As in, you made your bed,
Go lie in it,)

To be just like that,
Even go hide the same way, but
When it came right down to it,

I did something else instead.

Still.

PAINKILLERS

24.   A Prayer For Doubt

Rolled Lord,

Unknowable Lord,
Because doubt he's the things that
drives us
From what we know to
Court we do not know,
That her grandfather's doubt,
So that we may come to know
you better.

Lured helpless to see the ladies
That the things we call holy
Art instruments of the devil
In as much as the widest and most
prevalent DeVille
Requires the most disinterested virtue
to sustain it

O Lord help us to be certain that
Because Jesus Christ died for all are
seen
We can never know that we have
reason
For another soul to die.
Lord help us to know that doubt
He's begotten by feeder
And in feeder is a creature knowledge
of God.

Will Lord smile on the

As we smile on the humor
And foolishness of our own will
intentioned.

PAINKILLERS

25.   Walking Out Before April

Him out of the day with the patches of
blue along her eyes
And the trunks of the treaty;
looked like,
To the interest in the benefit coming
down from this guy.
I can hear the sound of the water from
yesterday's
Reign gurgling down me into the
drains...
The ground is like us
upon the overlook,
The next-door neighbor has hung small
plastic Easter
Ornaments from the
dogwood tree in his front yard.
In the end, all the houses with bleach,
And barns for all the cars
vs. medical wood,
With the activities in mind.

And we call ourselves to masters of the
universe, to this ice hot
and hot again with stories.
We all are what,
instruments of perverse fate!
Was like to grapple with a torch
to Longwood,
On two weeks march to Wheaton,
To hold us and we probably clown
When the wind flies past our feathers,

And what do we wish for them?
We wish for something green and
We wish for something
other than what we are.
We wish for something browsing and
We wish for something Lauren's...
Should and horror do you like a
brand?

Will and here's a dog market
for quickly, as a dog marching will
make poetry to alcohol.
Will all the recording him, or all I was,
What is the what that comes out me
like a computer
To work with a tough?
But he was in an even mean
to be written in,
The him with him, the what of him.
He was a very mean dog,
Being a glimpse
of forces the abundance,
Ready to make themselves yellow.

All my gosh it has been so cool for
weeks, for months it has been cold,
And I wonder
how many dogs there are.
And I wonder if the dogs wonder how
many people there are.
That was an airplane with use.
The airplane interfered with recording
as much as the dog did.

When I think this is enough,
I think this is enough. Words inch,
To put him into a politically minded
computer.

PAINKILLERS

25.   **Dragon Training**

The car is slicing through the night
and the nose of the car
is piercing the night like a knife.
The road is black
and there's a yellow stripe
down the middle of the road.
I aim at the point
where the road comes together
in the distance.
Beyond that point, I am aware
that there is more road there than
I know about.
There's a little bit of rain
and a little bit of fog
tonight.
By and large
visibility is quite acceptable.
There are cars coming
from the opposite direction
towards us,
but fortunately I don't have
my high beams on
so I don't have to worry
about blinding the drivers
in these oncoming cars.

Grace has a cold.
She coughs from time to time
and when she coughs
it makes me wonder again
if it will be recorded

on the tape recorder.
I wonder which file this is.
I think it must be a new file
even though the little screen
doesn't say that it is.
I think that light is red.
When the light is red,
that means it is time to stop the car.
When the light is green,
that means we can let the car go
forward again.
It looks like the light is
just about to turn green
and there it goes.
Here we go
off into the dark night again.
I'm going to have to put
my high beams on when I do this.
It makes the fog appear
a little more clearly
in front of my headlights.
We are driving
through Harding and New Vernon.
These are places where
there are very many wealthy people
living.
I hope they are happy
it is not a very cold night tonight.
I hope I don't drive
my car too fast,
because if I do
it may spin off the road.
        Emergency number:

Other emergency number:
This is a good way
to make a list.
I see reflectors
along the side of the road
next to the white line
that is painted there.
These reflectors may be dislodged
by the blade of the snowplow
during the cold winter months.
I remember
when I was living in California
these reflectors were
stuck into the roadside
almost everywhere you went.

PAINKILLERS

26.   Try Hard To Be Different

Live in the extreme outer reaches of
Subjectivity, push
The edge of what convention is
Prepared
To accept,
Look each person in the eye,
Listen for contra-
Dictions (there are no
contradictions except
In language),
Think of money
As something you give not
Something you have to spend,
Don't eat too much,
don't use things
You put into your own body
To alter the way
you think on purpose,
And sing as much as
Possible, especially
When you can sing
Together.

PAINKILLERS

27.   The Calf

(Exodus 32, 17-20)
When Joshua heard
The noise of the people shouting,
He said to Moses,
There is a noise of war
in the camp—
And Moses said,
It is not the voice
Of them that shout
for mastery,
Neither is it the voice
Of them that cry for being overcome:
I hear the noise of them
that are singing.
And it came to pass,
When Moses came nigh
unto the camp,
He saw the calf, and the dancing.
His anger waxed hot,
And he cast the tablets
out of his hands,
And broke them
beneath the mount.
And he took the calf
which they had made
And burned it in the fire,
And ground it to powder,
And scattered it upon the water,
And made the children of Israel
drink of it.

PAINKILLERS

28.   A Bump In The Night

I stood there watching the moon
Far, far away in the sky
So still, so white, so perfectly round
Against the black empty --

And it dawned on me:
That moon is just a bump
Sticking out
From that big flat wall called space
We comfort ourselves we belong in.

(But we don't).

Then suddenly
I felt my soul upwelling, outpouring,
Trailing tears like chains of diamonds;
And my soul met the moon
And held it close like in a cup
In the warm dark embrace of my heart
of hearts;
So that ever after neither my soul
Nor the moon's body
Nor any other thing
known or unknown
In the universe,
Was a part and not whole.

Now at night when I close my eyes to
sleep,
That pure open eye
Bathes my brain from within --

A living pearl of light;

And I am you, the same way.

29.   **Driving Home**

The light from the oncoming car
Seeps out from a pinpoint and
Spreads across the blotter of the dusk

As seen through my windshield
By me, on my way home
February first I think
In the year of our lord
Two thousand and something

It's coming

A cylindrical, blunt shadowshape
With highlights of gray airbrush
Fading into black
Lazily vaulting end over end
Slow, inevitable
Under the white hole of the moon
In a sky empty as enamel.

It's getting bigger
It's filling up the whole windshield
It's on me now like glue

No, not like glue, it missed,
It just missed me. I'm okay.
Until next time, I'm really okay.

Hey it's just something like that
flying saucer concrete chunk cookie

shaped
blood clot eyeball poking heart attack
again.

30.   Hannah

After all the therapies
But before the tumor in her head
finally got her
Joe and Diane took Hannah
To Florida so she could
Play with a dolphin
Before she died.

I like to think of her sitting in
The nice warm water
With her hands resting gently
On the slippery gray skin of
The creature's back,
As it held itself obediently
Suspended
And they exchanged sentient
awareness.

O Hannah, wherever you are,
I think you and the dolphin and the
water
And the pool of my thinking
And the voice of my calling,
We are all resting gently
Like your innocent hands
In the ocean of God.

PAINKILLERS

31.   **Closing The Book**

Every morning he stands by the bed
On his way out the door to work
Addressing her prone form,
holding a slim paperback
book of poems in his hands
He reads something of his choosing
Over the drone of the teevee voices
Usually short and to the point
Not thoroughly researched beforehand
In order to maintain
an air of spontaneity
So at the end it still seems like a gift
And she always acknowledges
the words
With a few muffled comments
before he bends
Brushing her lips with his,
And leaves for the day.

It must be a need he has
To get past the time in his childhood
When after three years of reading
Anything he liked even encyclopedias
Like the Book of Knowledge,
Between the ages of four and six
His father had intervened,
to assure that
He would grow up
knowing about work:
Work on the farm, and later in life
He would know work with his hands

He would work early and late
Every day would have
its portion of work
He would work and obey
as he was told
And so for his father's sake
He went forth to work not in vineyards
Nor in sheepfolds,
nor temple nor marketplace
But in cowbarns and chickenhouses
Where he hid books and stole time
To read them like a drunk
Hides bottles
and steals time to drink them.

So today, before he passes
that threshold
Again in miniature reiteration
of the original falling
From the grace of his childhood world
Redolent of virtual cloves and oranges
Awash in
sparkling spray off green waves
Troubled
by imaginary Mediterranean gusts
Charged with shafts of amber
and violet light
Past tall pillars in echoing chambers,
He stands and pays tribute to the
world created:
Imagination's empire made tangible,
By reading words about
love like a builder

Laying the groundworks for a bridge
From the limit of his mind
across to another
From the illusion of now to the
kingdom of then
From the broken to the whole.

PAINKILLERS

32.   About This Book

Someday
you may find yourself
standing at the edge
of a very deep hole
in the back yard of your head
and in the manner of Thomas De
Quincey
bowing down in his dream
before the lion
willing to be eaten,
you will pitch yourself forward
headlong into it.

Some people fall for a along time,
maybe forever,
and some people hit the bottom of that
hole, coming to their senses
or what is left of their senses
way down there in the dark.

The poems in this book
are pieces, shards, stones, little sticks,
with messages scratched into the
surface, for you to eke out meaning
in the dim light
and inform yourself,
should you ever
find yourself in that
place.

PAINKILLERS

33. A Higher Authority

Some people are determined
To arrive at their own understanding
with God
Without having any priest or church
Tell them how they should do it.

I have noticed that these people
Once they find themselves in the saved
condition
Are the ones most likely
To obey self appointed spiritual
guardians
Telling them what to do and what not
to do
Who to vote for, etc.

And they are also quickest to condemn
Others who may have different ideas.

PAINKILLERS

35. Ladysmith

Go ahead madam,
Take the handle of the hammer
in your hand.
If you want to understand what we do,
Swing the hammer for a moment
to and fro,
Just like this,

and imagine your arm
Swinging in an arc, wider,
until
He comes in a circle
up over from behind
And his head comes down
sharp and sure
Towards that flat part
on the anvil there;
But now, at this moment
when he is about to strike,
Hold him back,
as if you knew that by thinking so
You could have the metal
meet the metal
With no sound,
like the paw of a cat
Restraining a mouse
for her pleasure.

Yes madam,
In this way we dance
while we do sing,

PAINKILLERS

From all these years been pried away
From how many places
used to call our home,
Sent in crowds down
under the veldt into the dark,
Sweating out the gold,
breathing in the dust,
Until we wear the tunnels
on our skins;
So at night,
under the fractured slivers
of God's glory,
Hiding away from
their glimmering memory,
In the company house,
with no stars above us
Except in the mind's eye,
we join hands,
Dance, and sing, but gingerly,
so that our feet
Don't wake the white man
from his rest,
And our song not betray
wild raging under
The steady tread
and sheen of church harmonies.

And yes madam,
So does the big company
take out the gold,
Not thinking twice
about the blood and sweat
And the skin absorbing

the tunnels' spirit into itself,
But as if the tip of his pick
could strike the rock
Without any sound,
and the gold appear by magic
In long ingots
 resting in another vault,
who knows
How they got there?

And madam, dear lady,
Is this not like the story
of my namesake Joseph
Who entered the myth
having fathered
Yet not fathered,
our common redemption
from toil, injustice,
forced silence, sin,
and the dark?

PAINKILLERS

Adynaton:
The World Turned Upside Down

First appearing in the works of Virgil, this idea characterizes the excesses of the present age by stating a series of impossibilities.

"Pigs fly, horses talk, stars go dark, mountains fall into the sea."

In our age, technology has inured us to the miraculous. There are few, if any, cosmic contradictions. And yet we retain in our thinking certain moments that express a deep divide between what we do and what we think we want.

This piece explores three of these moments:

PAINKILLERS

37.   The Lepers

(In medieval times, lepers fastened
bells to their crutches so that those not
afflicted would hear their approach
and avoid them. This part expresses
the way that we try to place the
greatest distance between ourselves
and those who most need our help.)

Hear us
Hear us.

We warn you, we are coming

We do not warn you with a mighty
weapon
We have no weapon

We do not warn you with a coat of
mail
We have no armor but our skin

We do not warn you with a mask of
anger,
Only what is left of our faces

This fist cannot strike you
This foot cannot oppress you

We burn in our own slow fire

So hear us, hear us

PAINKILLERS

We ask you, hear us with your ears
See us with your eyes

In your eyes we search for pity
Not for anger, not for fear

In your eyes the cooling depth
Of mercy, pity, peace and love

Just see us with your eyes
As we pass along this highway

See us, hear us, touch us
Let our weakness perfect your strength

38. The Floating Island

(This part expresses our need to realize the remotest place as the happiest. As we heedlessly change the weather on earth, we dream of colonizing Mars.)

In Lydia there is a certain lake
In the mountains ever blue and high
And at its middle does an island make
The iris of a giant eye

By the shore, men and women stand
And to the water spirits daily call
Until in answer rises up the land
Floating in the sky above them all

Come now they cry, our joy complete
Leave your melancholy and your fears,
Come to the island in our little boat
We will rise and live among the stars.

PAINKILLERS

39. Today

(This part expresses the way that we allow fantasies to preoccupy us instead of stepping forth to take tangible action.)

Today, before you pass beyond
your threshold
Reiterating small
the first time falling,
Before you shed the grace
of childhood visions
Redolent of cloves
and virtual oranges,
Awash in sparkling
spray off dark green waves
Troubled by imaginary gusts,
Charged with wavering
shafts of amber light
And slender pillars
high in echoing chambers,
And so pay tribute
to the world created:
Imagination's empire
standing tangible.

Sing now words of love,
build like a builder,
Lay groundworks now to build
the greatest bridge:
Build from the edge of yourself
to another soul

Make of the broken illusion
something whole.

The Tower

(Three poems about towers.)

PAINKILLERS

41. Ugolino

When morning came, I saw
The faces of my children
Sleeping in the light
I saw they looked like me
I wept and cried aloud
And fearing they would wake
I bit into my finger...

But they had heard my cry
And when they saw the blood
They came to me and said
You bit yourself from hunger
O father father please
We are so hungry, please
Help us, help us die...

Our pain will go away
If you will kill us now
And you can eat our flesh
And drink our blood and live
Our pain will go away
And you will live longer
You will live longer
You will live
You will
You

PAINKILLERS

42. Chidiok Tichborne

This wall of stone is
       nothing more than air
And all of time and space before me lie
For if in future age some souls there be
Who little know my circumstance
       or care
Yet read these words and hear
       my music true
Then I can rest, for I will still be there.

PAINKILLERS

43.   Rapunzel

If I were to cut my golden hair
And braid a golden rope
And hang it from this hook
And climb down to the flow'ry
meadow

Would I be free, would I be, free?

If I were to leave this tower forever
And wander far away
Singing as I sing now
Searching the whole world over

Would I be free, would I be, free?

Yes, there are always three wishes
The third wish this must be
I wish I could know one who hears me
And what does that one see?

Then I would be free,
Then I would be free.

PAINKILLERS

44. My Eyes

My eyes are killing me,
O God, my eyes are killing me!

When you made these eyes for me
O God you made these eyes to see…

Right now I'd like to put them out
Get something else to fill their spot

Now I don't care if I can see
Because I'm trying to get free

Because my eyes are killing me,
My eyes are killing me.

PAINKILLERS

45. Why I Love My Scars

If I turn my forearm to the side,
just like this,
I can see a little bump.

It's all that's left of the time
And I put my arm up to stop the stone
Before it hit my face.

I didn't stop them all.

A stick with a pointy end
Made it through to my cheek,

Plenty of other stuff made it through;
Stuff that didn't leave any scars.

But the scars are good.

If I try to remember what really
happened 45 years ago
There's always some doubt
That what I remember is the same.

The scars are evidence.
Those things really happened.
I'm not making this up.

The scars are the truth.

The scars are not ugly,
they are beautiful.

Something has to be in here about how
looking at the scars makes me feel.

Scars are actually the last thing it takes
to make a person perfect.

I mean, you go through your life,
you're trying to do something with
yourself, improve yourself, all that.

Think about it. In the French language
the word blessed means mortally
wounded.

Why is that? Did they think you were
closer to God
when you were about to die?

Jesus didn't hesitate
to show off his scars,
and he went into heaven
with them still on.

I like to think he has them right now,
And every once in a while
Looks at them
with something like gratitude.

46.   **The Vision of Ezekiel**

I looked above and saw a stormy wind
draw down the dark across the northern sky,
and a great cloud, all shot with brightness, came
filled with fire and flashing from within,
and the flames of glory gleamed like amber.
And in the fire were living creatures four.
These creatures that I saw had human form,
each one had faces four, and each four wings.

In the front I saw a human face
and a lion's face along the right,
and an ox's face along the left,
and an eagle looking from the back.
Each creature had two wings spread out above,
There were two more wrapt around their bodies,
and they rested one wing on another.
Under their wings, each one had human hands.

These living creatures darted to and fro.
Each figure moved ahead, and did not turn:
where the spirit took them, they did go.

PAINKILLERS

In the middle of the living creatures
something looked like burning coals of fire,
it moved like torches moving to and fro
among the living creatures, bright like fire,
with lightning flashes from inside the fire.

The creatures' legs were straight, feet were cleft
like calves feet; they shone like burnished bronze.
And as I saw them go, these living creatures,
awesome wheels began to turn beside them.
There was one wheel for each of them the four.
The wheels were like the gleaming of a beryl;
and the four wheels were all of them like made,
each like a wheel that turned within a wheel.

And when they moved, they moved in any way,
but did not veer from true as on they went.
Of these wheels, the rims were tall and awesome,
for the rims were full of eyes all round.
The wheels did turn beside the living creatures,
and as the living creatures rose above me,
the wheels rose also, on and on they went,

and the living creatures' life was in them.
There was a space above us like a dome,
shining with cut stones and walls of crystal.
When the creatures moved, I heard a sound,
a sound like living ocean in their wings.
I heard the thunder of the God Almighty!
A mighty sound that drove away all sound!
A sound of tumult like a raging army
Fighting and dying in the dome above us!

And then I saw a the likeness of a throne,
and something like a human form appeared
seated on this likeness of a throne.
Blue, like a sapphire, living light it was,
and there was splendor, splendor all around!
My eyes were blinded by the light of heaven,
My ears made deaf by all the tumult there!
And so I slept, and wept when I awoke.

PAINKILLERS

LYRICS

PAINKILLERS

There Is No Age

In 2005, Harmonium Choral Society of Morristown, NJ, celebrated their 25th Anniversary by commissioning composer Edie Hill to write a piece that would express how people in the chorus felt during the time they were actually singing. I asked the singers to describe their feelings, and wrote an assemblage of their thoughts into this poem. A recording of this work was featured on National Public Radio's "All Things Considered" in January, 2006, in one of the most popular segments ever aired on the NPR show.

I have a flower in my heart
Like a rose
It opens, how it opens
No one knows

We can see beyond the walls
Until there are no walls
Beyond horizons
The infinite calls

It is not an emptiness
We enfold it
Raising high our hearts
Behold it

PAINKILLERS

You will find us
In the tuning of our breath
Past all knowing of another
Or life, or death

And we will hear your voice
In what was always there
And so be one with you
Everywhere

There is no age
No bending of the stem
No ending of the song
No requiem

I have a flower in my heart
Come see
It opens, and we call it
Harmony

Song of Childhood

i.

We built that summer day
With bales of hay

We tilled that autumn dust
With trees of rust

We swept that winter night
With wounds of white

And then the field,
The field beneath the bud,
Made little leaves on tips of trees,
Leaves the color of blood.

ii.

The larch against the sky
Lashes the moon's eye

The feathers lost in the field
Symbols yield

The moth eclipsing the flame
Declares your name.

And now the sky,
The source beyond the dark,
Sings a song of love unfolding,
Of mystery the mark.

PAINKILLERS

Daughter Of Rage

She was the baby they almost lost--
She loved to ride horses
and dance on the stage.
She had it all coming,
whatever the cost--
She was their daughter,
the daughter of rage.

Daughter of rage doesn't bother to worry
Has it already and still has to hurry
To find her romances, take her own chances
And fly through the gathering storm.

When she was four
Daddy walked out the door--
She held to her Mommy
and stared at the sky--
As she got older
she tried lots of shoulders
Looking for love and new places to cry.

Some are born happy
and some are born sad,
Some spend a lifetime
locked up in a cage.
Some learn to tell
the good from the bad,
One in a lifetime's
a daughter of rage.

PAINKILLERS

The Heart Of Your Song

I had a dream
A dream that still lingers
I saw a heaven
A heaven apart
The air of your spirit
Flowed down through my fingers
And wrapped a tight bud
In the rose of my heart

So hold me, hold me
Enfold me all night long
Hold me, hold me
Deep in the heart of your song

We sang the glory,
all of the glory
The sweetest sad story
We ever were told
My sky was your song
All through the night long
It bundled my heart
In chords of gold

So hold me, hold me
Enfold me all night long
Hold me, hold me
Deep in the heart of your song

PAINKILLERS

O Fish

O fish, green fish
Are you a part of this water?

O bird, blue bird
Are you a part of this air?

O worm, pink worm
Are you a part of this earth?

O moth, white moth
Are you a part of this flame?

O note, clear note
Are you a part of this music...

These are things
I see with my eyes
My eyes see me seeing them, too.

PAINKILLERS

Cynthia Departing

Cynthia departing wore a cape
Of pearl-gray silk and lace;
As we kissed her breath was sweet
And warm along my face.

How many times I see her shape
Vanish in the mist at last,
Leaving to linger, at my feet
Rose shadows that her cape has cast.

PAINKILLERS

Song of the Dancer

I will not tell you who I am
    With words, words, words.
Look for me flying in the air
    With birds, birds, birds.
How can I think of soaring as I wish
Chasing, and embracing,
    my bright vision,
When I must follow black,
    quotidian footprints,
Locked in place by
    hybrid mathematician?

My teacher always says to me,
    "Technique! Technique!"
Even the larks must serenade
    with beak, beak, beak.
My soul is trapped in ice, a winter fish
Asleep in some
    suspended animation;
O dream about propellers,
    rudders, wings
Far above the world's
    concatenation.

PAINKILLERS

I Have A Dream

I have a dream…
I know we will find a way
Yes there will come a day
When we see equality

I have a dream
We come from near or far
Judge us by who we are
Not race or bigotry

I have a dream
Children throughout this land
All standing hand in hand
From sea to shining sea

CHORUS

Dream with me now
I'll show you how
Dream with me now
I'll show you how

PAINKILLERS

It's Our World

It's our world

We have to watch over it
We have to take care of it
It's our world

It's so beautiful
Fish in the blue blue sea
Birds in the blue blue sky
It's so beautiful

We are tomorrow
Let's face it together
Let's all help each other
We are tomorrow

It's our world
And our tomorrow is now

PAINKILLERS

Come Now Ye Wealthy
(James 5, 1-6)

Come now ye wealthy weep and wail
In your sorrow and your pain
Your riches all gone rank and stale
Your robes becaked with soil and stain

Your gold and silver flaked with rust
And all your treasure crushed and lost
Your follies scattered in the dust
Like flesh within a furnace toss'd.

You laid your gold up in a tower
Stolen from the poor man's labor
Took by fraud and stealth and power
Slave and stranger, friend and
neighbor.

So now goes up the reaper's cry
To the ear of God on high:
Hast thou choked on luxury
While lesser folk lay starving by?

Hast thou fattened yet your heart
From your brimming dish of gore?
Murder'd thou the better part
Who may resist you ever more!

PAINKILLERS

Piano Pieces
By Johannes Brahms

I.   Prufrock's Reverie (From "The
Love Song Of J. Alfred Prufrock,"
by T. S. Eliot)

In the room the women come and go
Talking of Michelangelo.

They shift their silkclad thighs
Along the thick brocade;
They heave their great sad sighs
For grease monkeys in the motor trade.

Their thick plaits fall and swing,
Dangling in idle grace;
They dream of a thing
       that is not a thing
In a place that is not a place.

In the room the women come and go
Talking of Michelangelo.

II. Reuben's Reverie (From "Roger
Malvin's Burial," by Nathaniel
Hawthorne)

Oh who, in the enthusiasm
of a daydream,
has not wished that he
were a wanderer
in a world of summer wilderness,
with one fair
and gentle hanging lightly on his arm?

In youth his free and exulting step
would know no barrier
but the rolling ocean or
the snow-topped mountains;
calmer manhood would choose a home
where Nature had strewn
a double wealth
in the vale of some transparent stream;
and when hoary age,
after long, long years
of that pure life,
stole on and found him there,
it would find him the father of a race,
the patriarch of a people,
the founder
of a mighty nation yet to be.

When death,
like the sweet sleep which we welcome
after a day of happiness,
came over him,
his far descendants
would mourn over the venerated dust.

Enveloped by tradition
in mysterious attributes,
the men of future generations
would call him godlike;
and remote posterity
would see him standing,
dimly glorious,
far up the valley
of a hundred centuries.

III.   The Echo Of
         The Song Of Songs

On my bed at night I sought him!
On my bed at night I sought him!

Who my heart loves!
Who my heart loves!

I sought him but I did not find him!
I sought him but I did not find him!

I will rise then and go about the city!
I will rise then and go about the city!

In streets and crossings I will seek him!
In streets and crossings I will seek him!

Who my heart loves!
Who my heart loves!

IV.   De Quincey's Reverie
        (From "Suspiria De Profundis")

Out of the darkness
if I happen to call back
the image of Fanny
Up rises suddenly
from a gulf of forty years
a rose in June
or if I think for an instant
of the rose in June,
up rises the heavenly face of Fanny.

One after the other
like the antiphonies in a choral service
rise Fanny and the rose in June
then back again
the rose in June and Fanny.

Then come both together as in a chorus
roses and Fannies, Fannies and roses,
without end, thick
as blossoms in Paradise.

V.   Reverie Of The Rich Man
        (From the Epistle of James)

And if a brother or sister be naked
and in want of daily food
and one of you say to them,
"Go in peace, be warmed and filled"

Yet you do not give them
what is necessary for the body,
what does it profit?
Faith without work is dead in itself --

Show me thy faith without works:
I from my works
will show thee my faith.

Thou believest there is one God --
thou dost well.
The devils also believe, and tremble.

VI.   The Worst That Could Happen
        (From "The Man Of
        The Crowd," by E. A. Poe)

There are some secrets which
do not permit themselves to be told

men die nightly in their beds
wringing the hands of ghostly
confessors,

looking them piteously in the eyes

die with despair of heart
and convulsion of throat
because of mysteries
known only to themselves
which do not suffer themselves to be
revealed,

and thus
the essence of all crime
is undivulged, a mystery,
without a name or place.

Dog Boy

Hey Dog Boy --
Let me be your jaw toy,
Show you how to meat choke,
Need a cheap stroke, Dog Boy,
What ha-a-a-ave you done?

Hey Dog Boy --
Show me some raw joy,
Tell me 'bout that phone pole,
Sniffin' round that bone hole, Dog Boy,
What ha-a-a-ave you done?

Hey Dog Boy -- come and get it!
Exercise your tongue, boy!
Deep sniffin' on the raunchy haunch,
Quick lickin' at the lucky lunch,
Dog Boy, What ha-a-a-ave you done?

PAINKILLERS

Treating People Like Objects

Have you seen my finial?
I press it in, erupting up
To the unspoken, thrusting cup,
The broken cusping of the curve
Embraced by straitened leaves above,
The glossy doors, the case beneath
Holding its breath of hormones sweet,
Braiding of tighter hair the wreath
That in these shades we might beget
An elegant mahogany.

Have you held my hair receiver?
The china of its nesting lid,
Normal best, of louse-nits rid,
My brushes bursting with their burn
Of brass against the coiling fern;
And down against her curl of leg
Rages my certain, cylindric bliss,
For all our cloaks the furtive peg:
Protract in time the circular kiss
Into our oral custody.

Have you pierced the darker glass?
Its eye contains the sloping weight
Of flesh suspended from the heart,
The twisting channel of the worm
Intent upon its world apart;
The blades my shoulder will not yield
Have slit the earth like furtive plows,
So come, Receiver of the Seed,
To bind our oath with solemn vows
Of reticent modernity.

Song of the Lover

Only my edge-of-your-eyelid's kiss
Could open your eyes
To show you how perfect perfect
darkness is.

Love is a cloud
Moist in the air
Poised on the edge
Of heaven's dome.

Love is an arc
Traced by a leaf
Red as a boat
In its watery home.

Love is a house
Ringed by a moat
A house of sand waiting
For tides, for tides to come.

This room, this place is ours now.
Now close your eyes.
Hear them, the seas and skies, singing.